Growing and Showing
Chrysanthemums

Wallace Brook

David & Charles
Newton Abbot   London   North Pomfret (Vt)

Photographs by Michael Kelly and Wallace Brook
Line illustrations by Eric Brooks

British Library Cataloguing in Publication Data

Brook, Wallace
    Growing and showing chrysanthemums. –
    (Growing and showing)
    1. Chrysanthemums
    I. Title   II. Series
    635.9'3355   SB413

    ISBN 0–7153–8574–7

Photoset in Souvenir by
Northern Phototypesetting Co, Bolton
and printed in Great Britain by
Redwood Burn Ltd, Trowbridge, Wilts
for David & Charles (Publishers) Limited
Brunel House   Newton Abbot   Devon

Published in the United States of America
by David & Charles Inc
North Pomfret   Vermont 05053   USA

Contents

1 Aims and Decisions

Chrysanthemum growing for exhibition is the finest antidote to work that I know, and a great test of character – that is if you aim to win when you put your flowers on the show bench. Determination, dedication, perseverance and patience are all necessary qualities if you are going to reach the top. I am firmly convinced that the chrysanthemum as a flower offers a much greater challenge to the exhibitor than any other species, though I do admit to a certain bias! My chrysanthemums are also a relaxation therapy, an occupation at all times of year, which gives the pleasure of observing, and being involved with, the changing seasonal patterns.

Earlies, Lates or Both?

Do you grow earlies or do you grow lates? I knew one grower who had a garden of approximately 14.5sq m (17½sq yd) and a greenhouse of about 6.5sq m (8sq yd), grew about 40 earlies and 20 lates, with tremendous enthusiasm and dedication, and won many a prize at the local shows. To grow both is a practical proposition provided you have a garden and greenhouse; the number of plants you grow is determined by the area of your ground and the size of the greenhouse. Earlies and lates for exhibition are grown with an average of 5 plants per sq m (10sq ft).

If you are concerned about the time factor, or holidays, you can generally say that earlies are less demanding than lates. The early grower's season starts about mid-January and is virtually completed by the end of September; your stock will not be harmed by your absence for a couple of weeks in January or February or when you have planted out in the middle of May. The late grower's season starts about Christmas time and he is similarly placed in the early part of the year, and again after final potting in May or June, a couple of weeks away from the plants will do them no harm. The October break that is often taken by the early grower is not really advised for the dedicated late exhibitor, unless you have a really proficient caretaker-grower available.

5

The majority of successful exhibitors are part of a team, for to win a large national class is often beyond the reach of an individual working alone, from rooting to putting the blooms on the show bench. I have the finest assistant in an understanding wife who helps at show time and does all the necessary jobs when I am out.

If you do not have a greenhouse, forget the lates and concentrate on earlies. You can grow these to exhibition standards by importing your plants each year from a reliable source, putting them into a cold frame around early March, and from there moving them straight into the outside bed.

Classification: The Various Types

The National Chrysanthemum Society, over innumerable years, has classified the various cultivars as they have become available to the grower, automatically placing them in one of 28 different sections. We, as exhibitors, are concerned with three groups of chrysanthemums:

Outdoor cultivars or *earlies* (sections 23 to 30)
These generally flower outside in the open before 1 October without any protection. They are shown in August, September and October.

Indoor cultivars or *lates* (sections 1 to 12)
These are generally flowered with greenhouse protection in November for exhibition in that month, but can be flowered to show in October or as cut flowers in December.

October flowering group (sections 13 to 20)
These may be shown as earlies or lates in August, September, October and November.

Many people, including the majority of our top exhibitors, have a preference for a certain type of flower and specialise in growing this one type. The seven different types of flower that concern us at this stage are:

Incurved (sections 3, 13 and 23)
These are spherical in form with florets pointing towards the centre of the crown, or whorling to a bloom without gaps and depressions in its floret lay.

Fig 1 Different types of chrysanthemum: a) intermediate; b) single; c) incurved; d) reflexed

Reflexed (sections 4, 14 and 24)
These have florets which reflex outwards and downwards to give an outline which shows breadth and depth in equal proportion.

Intermediate (sections 5, 15 and 25)
These are blooms of varying characteristics. They stand between the incurved and the reflexed and should be generally globular in outline.

Singles (sections 7, 17 and 27)
These have approximately five rows of ray florets with a circular disc in the centre.

Anemones (sections 6 and 26)
These have highly developed tubular disc florets forming a dome-shaped cushion.

Sprays (sections 9, 19 and 29)
These are flowering growths with six to thirty blooms on pedicels emerging from the main stem.

Large and medium exhibitions (sections 1 and 2)
Classified only according to size and colour, and not to form.

Flower size
The incurves, reflexes, intermediates, singles and anemones are subdivided into large-flowered (a), medium-flowered (b) and small-flowered (c). Some top exhibitors tend to grow either large or medium cultivars so as to have a better chance on the show bench. Forget about the small-flowered at this stage, as there are not many around.

Colours
There is also a colour classification to assist growers, though it does not always give the precise colour. The key is:

W White	P Pink	B Bronze	
C Cream	DP Deep pink	DB Deep bronze	
LY Light yellow	LS Light salmon	LR Light red	Pu Purple
Y Yellow	S Salmon	R Red	DPu Deep purple
DY Deep yellow	DS Deep salmon	DR Deep Red	O Other colours
LP Light pink	LB Light bronze	LPu Light purple	(green, etc)

To explain all this official chrysanthemum jargon let us take a couple of cultivars as examples:

Arnold Fitton 1 Pu. This means that Arnold Fitton is a large exhibition cultivar, classified section 1, ie late. It is purple and can be exhibited at October and November shows.

Ann Brook 23b Y. This is an early incurved cultivar. It is yellow and can be shown only as a (b), ie medium-flowered, at August, September and October shows.

Which Show?

When you have decided between earlies or lates, the next question is which show or shows you are aiming for. Is it to be your local show just down the road, probably run by the local horticultural society; the show of the nearest specialist chrysanthemum society; the nearest National Chrysanthemum Society Group show (the groups are Northern, Midland, Welsh, Scottish and Southern); or the NCS National show at Westminster?

If you are just starting off you will probably be growing a few medium- and a few large-flowered earlies of various types – incurves, reflexes and intermediates. Fair enough: you are now equipped to compete at local, or even Group, level – possibly even at national level. There are classes at all these shows for the small grower, as well as for the specialist who competes in the premier classes and is likely to be specialising in either medium or large flowers. You will be able to specialise when you find out which you grow best – or, should I say, which do best for you on the show bench.

Similarly with lates: if you are starting out, you will be growing a few incurves, a few decoratives (reflexed and intermediate), a few singles and maybe the odd few large exhibitions. You can decide which you prefer to grow when you get used to the various types. A few red cards (first prizes) will do wonders for your morale, and it is quite common for a novice grower to produce the goods in his first year of growing.

Always try to have a target, aim for a certain show. Even if you don't get there you should have gained invaluable experience in the attempt. Never be afraid of going for the top: remember the old proverb, 'faint heart never won fair maiden'.

2 Selecting Cultivars and Stock

Once your target is defined, a certain amount of thought has to go into the selection of cultivars for that particular show. You have to know your cultivars and you have to know their approximate flowering time. Some earlies flower naturally during August, some are much later in flowering, say about the end of September. Obviously it is useless growing August flowering earlies for late September shows! Similarly with lates: it is hopeless to grow cultivars that reach their best at the end of November for shows held during the last week in October.

A novice grower may wonder how to find out which cultivars flower when. Your local chrysanthemum-society members will be able to fill you in with such facts, telling you which chrysanths have an early natural flowering time and which are late. The National Chrysanthemum Society in its publications *Panorama* and *Year Book* gives an analysis of all the flowers shown at Westminster and also names the majority of prizewinning blooms at the Group shows (only available to NCS members and fellows). You also know the dates of all these shows, so you can soon see which cultivars perform best at certain dates. Specialist chrysanthemum firms generally put in their catalogues the recommended 'stopping' times for each cultivar they sell. Stopping is the art of pinching out the plant's growing point.

Taking earlies as an example, anything with an April stop is a natural late-flowering early; and those with end of May or June stops are early-flowering earlies. But probably the best bet would be to buy a small booklet called *Stopping Times* published by the NCS Northern Group, where all the relevant information on this issue is to be found (see page 61).

Rooting times are also a big help in determining the natural flowering time. Generally, the earlier the rooting date the later the flowering.

When you have sorted out the natural flowering times, you have to decide which are the best cultivars for the job in hand. Again find out which are the most popular cultivars at the shows; these are the ones to try. Have a word with a good amateur exhibitor and I feel sure you will get the advice you wish.

The following sections give recommended cultivars with colour classifications, recommended rooting times, stopping dates for central areas and my pot size for lates. For instance, 'Pink Duke LP, Dec–Jan, 20 May, 10in' means Pink Duke, colour classification light pink, rooting time December to January, stopping date 20 May, and final pot size 10in.

Recommended Earlies

Large flowered

Incurved:
Alison Kirk W, Jan, 20 April   Winnie Bramley Y, Feb, 5 May

Reflexed:
Formcast Pu, Jan–Feb, 5 May
Gambit Pu, Feb, 15 May   Miss World P, Jan, 20 April
Sam Oldham R, Jan, 20 April   Snowflake W, Dec–Jan, 1 April

Intermediate:
Ann Dickson LB, Jan, 20 April   Primrose Chessington LY,
Bill Wade W, Jan, 1 April   Jan, 15 April
Doreen Hall LP, Jan, 1 April   Apricot Chessington LB,
Chessington W, Jan, 15 April   Jan, 15 April

Medium flowered

Incurved:
Peter Rowe Y, Jan, 25 April
Woolmans Celebration W, Feb, 25 May

Reflexed:
Eve Gray PP, Feb, 25 May   Salmon Venice S, Jan, 25 April
Joyce Stevenson R, Feb, 20 May   Martina B, Feb, 5 May
Venice P, Jan, 25 April   George Griffiths DR, Jan, 5 May

11

Intermediate:

Cornish C, Jan, 25 April
Oyster LP, Jan, 20 April
Ginger Nut LB, Jan, 5 May

Yellow Ginger Nut Y, Jan, 5 May
Nora Brook LB, Jan, 20 April
Madge Welby LY, Jan–Feb, 5 May

Sprays

Root mid March and stop the end of May.
Margaret P, White Margaret W, Primrose Margaret LY, Marion PY,
Pennine Wine DR, Yellow Heide Y, Apricot Madeleine LB

Recommended Lates

Nat 1 = natural first crown, Nat 2 = natural second crown

Large exhibition

Pink Duke LP, Dec–Jan, 20 May, 10in
Gigantic S, Jan, 10 May, 9in or 10in
Silver Gigantic O, Jan, 15 May, 9in or 10in
Jessie Habgood W, Dec–Jan, 15 May, 10in
Harry Gee LP, Dec–Jan, 5 April and 10 June, 10in (second crown)
Shirley Primrose Y, Jan, Nat 1, 9in
Jimmy Mottram DS, Dec–Jan, 15 April, 9in

Medium exhibition

Lundy W, Jan, 25 May, 9in
Seychelle P, Dec–Jan, 15 April, 8½in or 9in
Idris S, Feb, 25 May, 9in
Cossack R, Jan, Nat 1, 8½in
Connie Mayhew Y, Dec–Jan, 10 March and 10 May, 8in or 8½in (second crown)

Large flowered

Incurved:

Shirley Sunburst Y, Feb, Nat 1, 8in or 8½in
Pelsall Imperial LB, Jan, 15 May, 8½in
Shirley Model P, Feb, Nat 1, 8in or 8½in

Reflexed:

Leicester W, Feb, Nat 1, 9in
West Bromwich W, March, 7 June, 9in or 10in

Intermediate:
Beacon R, Jan, 15 May, 9in
Sam Vinter W, Jan, 1 April and 8 June, 9in
Fair Lady P, Feb, 30 May, 9in or 10in
Orange Fair Lady LB, Feb, 10 June, 9in or 10in
Yellow Fair Lady Y, Feb, 10 June, 9in or 10in
Crimson Purple Glow R, Jan, 1 April and 1 June, $8\frac{1}{2}$in or 9in

Singles:
Woolmans Glory B, Jan, 1 April and 25 May, 8in or $8\frac{1}{2}$in
Red Woolmans Glory R, Jan, 1 April and 25 May, 8in or $8\frac{1}{2}$in
Golden Woolmans Glory Y, Jan, 1 April and 25 May, 8in or $8\frac{1}{2}$in
Annina Y, Jan, 1 April and 1 June, $8\frac{1}{2}$in or 9in

Medium flowered

Incurved:
Fairweather LPu, Feb, 20 May, $8\frac{1}{2}$in
White Fairweather W, Feb, 20 May, $8\frac{1}{2}$in
John Hughes W, Feb, Nat 1, 8in or $8\frac{1}{2}$in
Yellow John Hughes Y, Feb, Nat 1, 8in or $8\frac{1}{2}$in
Minstrel Boy LB, Feb, 1 June, 8in or $8\frac{1}{2}$in

Reflexed:
Beechview Flame B, Feb, 1 June, 9in
Regency Pu, Jan, 15 May, $8\frac{1}{2}$in or 9in
Xenia Noelle R, Feb, 15 June, $8\frac{1}{2}$in

Intermediate:
Winter Queen W, Jan, 1 May, 9in
Bill Holbrook W, March, Nat 1, 9in
Alfreton Cream C, Feb, Nat 1, 9in
Yellow Alfreton Cream Y, Feb, Nat 1, 9in

Singles:
My Love B, Feb, 1 April and 1 June, 8in or $8\frac{1}{2}$in
Masons Bronze B, Feb, Nat 2, $8\frac{1}{2}$in
Nancy Sherwood Y, Feb, Nat 2, $8\frac{1}{2}$in
Chesswood Beauty R, Feb, Nat 2, $8\frac{1}{2}$in

Sprays
Root early July and grow without stopping.
Romark W, Robeam Y, Pink Gin LPu, Roscene W, Rynoon LP, Ryflame B, Rytang B

The Record Book

It is essential for an exhibitor to keep a record book – quite often we see a really good vase of flowers produced by a novice as a one-off job, and then never again see a vase of a similar calibre from that exhibitor. This is really disappointing to the grower in question and completely disheartening; it can result in him giving up growing. If he (or she) had kept a complete record of all details relating to the growth of the plants, from rooting to cutting, he would stand a much greater chance of reproducing that vase.

I have seen record books in all forms: small notebooks, diaries, large hardbacked books which can hold records for about ten years, or even just single sheets of paper. It doesn't matter what form it takes as long as all the relevant information is there in black and white for future reference. My own record books go back for forty-five years, and have changed a great deal.

I generally start off with a complete list of all cultivars to be grown, with a section for lates, earlies and sprays. Next I put down the number of plants of each cultivar grown last season, and in the next column the number to be grown in the current season. With a little bit of arithmetic I can finalise numbers to be grown by a process of addition and amendment. These figures are really determined and finalised by the size of the early bed and greenhouse. The third column contains the rooting dates, followed by the stopping dates, and finally a large column for any comments during the growth period.

It has always been my practice to put labels in the pots, with the name of the cultivar, the rooting date, the stopping date, the compost mixture (A, B, C, etc) and the firmness of potting if it is a late (shown by an L for light potting, M for medium or H for hard). These could be in the record book, but I prefer to be able to see any flower's full history of culture at a glance. Invariably, I find myself with two or three mixes for final composts. These are written out in full on the next page of the record book and marked A, B, C, etc. Also written out in full, and in chronological order, are all the cultural routines and treatments performed during the season. These include spray applications, feeding, top dressing, counting down, weather patterns and any other important facts or details.

It is important I believe to put things down as soon as you have done them – or you will soon forget, and by the end of the season you won't have a clue as to what you did.

Stock Selection

The secret of successful growing for exhibition is attention to detail – it is of paramount importance at all times in our cultural year.

The first detailed point is stock selection or stock reselection. The good exhibitor demands that the plants he grows must be the offspring of plants that have produced superior flowers with good size, form and colour. It is only by insisting on this principle of culture that improvement can be maintained. At the end of the season all plants that have produced exceptionally good blooms should be marked in some way. I generally give really superior stock a label with four stars. Any a little below this standard of quality are given three stars, the next best two stars and the others one. All other stock and any plants that have produced substandard blooms are discarded or destroyed. It is no good propagating from such plants – this will eventually lead to inferior stock with inferior blooms.

Sources of Supply

At the start of the season your stock should be full of health and vigour, and the stool it came off should have produced top-quality flowers. If it is your first season of growing and you have no stock of your own to work with, alternative sources of supply will have to be explored.

If I was in this position, my first choice would be to approach a good amateur exhibitor who has shown good blooms of the cultivars I required, or who grows the type of chrysanthemum that I intend to grow. My next choice would be a specialist chrysanthemum raiser, preferably one who advertises his stock as heat-therapy treated. One or two firms now have plant-health units, designed to give stock plants which produce disease-free material to be distributed to their customers. The majority of these specialists advertise in the literature of the National Chrysanthemum Society.

The most common way to purchase new stock is in the form of rooted cuttings in the early part of the year, around February. Get your order in fairly early and ask for delivery about the time you require the plants. Another way is to order unrooted cuttings and grow a root system on them yourself. This is less expensive and quite satisfying, if you are fitted up for rooting.

3 Growing Earlies

Bearing in mind the last point of stock selection and making sure that all your four-star performers are marked, after flowering, burn all the sub-standard plants or put them in the dustbin, for in all probability there will be some form of disease on them. Just lift them out with the garden fork, shake off the soil and destroy them in one way or another.

It is now about mid to late October and the covers will still be on the beds. Don't be tempted to take them off, for the enemy of early-flowering stools is wetness coupled with cold. The covers will keep the old plants in a state which will not encourage too much basal growth if there is warmish weather and rain. They will also keep the moisture to a minimum if the weather is cold, stagnant and wet.

Cutting Down

The flowers will probably have been cut off in September and as the nights get shorter the sap flow in the remaining part of the plant known as the footstalk will lessen. In early to mid October the foot-stalks can be shortened to about half a metre in height. Later in the month, the footstalks can be reduced by anything up to 50 per cent. The cut ends will bleed less at this time than if cut earlier in the month; they will dry and heal fairly quickly ready for lifting in late October or even November.

Lifting and Boxing

Mix sufficient compost for boxing up your stools when lifted. John Innes No1 or No2 compost is ideal, and it should be moist but not too wet. Collect a stock of clean boxes similar to haddock–fillet boxes. They should be half as deep again as tomato trays, or twice as deep as seed trays. If they are old boxes make sure that they have been treated or washed with something similar to Jeyes Fluid solution and allowed to drain and dry off.

Lifting is quite simple if carried out with a garden fork. Take hold of the footstalk of the stool and shake off as much of the soil as you can – it will come off fairly easily if it is dry. Prune down all the basal growth with a pair of secateurs. Do not break it or pull it off with your hands or you will destroy the eyes and small pieces of stems that are going to produce your propagating material in a few weeks' time. Then take a large pair of scissors and prune back the roots to about a 50 or 75mm (2 or 3in) ball. Some growers then wash off the remaining soil to get rid of slug eggs, etc. Place the stools in the boxes on top of about 50mm (2in) of moist John Innes compost, packing them quite close together. Then add the same compost to cover the roots. Don't cover the crowns too much: I always find it better to have more compost below the roots than on top.

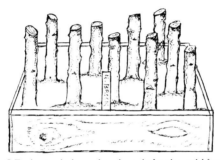

Fig 2 Early stools, boxed and ready for the cold frame

Cold Frame or Greenhouse?

When the stools are boxed they can go either into a cold frame or a cold greenhouse. Mine invariably go into the cold frame covered with frame lights, and I give them ventilation whenever possible. Don't let them dehydrate, but, on the other hand, don't let them get wet and cold or they will stagnate and develop botrytis, which appears as a fluffy mould and will ruin the stools. If you have to apply moisture, give plenty of ventilation so that it can dry off the surface.

I remember once receiving stools with hardly any root, in an envelope from Scotland. I thought they looked so dehydrated that they would give me no propagating material at all, but, to my surprise, they threw twenty-four cuttings after boxing, watering and heating!

Producing Propagating Material

Producing cuttings is comparatively easy. Take the boxes of stools into the slight warmth of the greenhouse, give them some bottom heat and a little moisture and they will appear without any trouble.

Not all earlies are put to root at the same time. The first to go in, during January, are the cultivars requiring a stop in April. The ones to be stopped in May are inserted around February and the June-stopped cultivars in early March. Generally, cuttings are put to root about fifteen weeks before stopping takes place. This should produce a good root system and build up the plant to the right condition for stopping at the required time.

With this in mind, I take the boxes of stools from the frame into the greenhouse and put them on a soil-warming cable on the bench at least a month, or even six weeks with the early ones, before I require the cuttings. With a bottom heat of 13° to 15°C (55° to 60°F) and a minimum air temperature of 5°C (40°F), cuttings will appear two or three weeks after watering (use a rosed can). Don't get the stools too wet before they have warmed through, and watch for aphids, which can run riot in such conditions. A good spray with an insecticide recommended for chrysanthemums will do the trick. If any botrytis appears on the stems, a fungicidal spray or a dusting with flowers of sulphur will prevent it from spreading into the cuttings at the base of the stools.

The Propagating Pit (earlies and lates)

Chrysanthemums root in virtually any medium, but do better in some than others. You want to put a root system on a small cutting

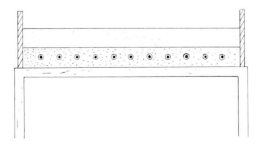

Fig 3 Section through a propagating pit on the greenhouse bench. The bottom layer of river sand holds the soil-warming cable, and the rooting compost lies on top. Both layers are 50mm (2in) deep

fairly quickly and have the root in such a condition that it will take to the next compost immediately. I make a propagating pit from a rectangular wooden frame about 2m (6ft 6in) long, by 1m (3ft 3in) wide, and 150mm (6in) deep. Place this on the bench in the greenhouse on a sheet of polythene, partially fill with 25mm (1in) of river sand, and then run out a 250 volt soil-warming cable, spacing it over the sand. Place another 25mm (1in) of river sand over the top of the cable and then 50mm (2in) of rooting compost over the sand.

Rooting Composts (earlies and lates)

I have rooted chrysanthemums for years in a compost made up with 1 part loam, 1 part granulated sphagnum peat and 1 part river sand. However, with the introduction of perlite, I can get much faster results with the following mix: 1 part loam (it may be sterilised to keep it weed free), 1 part peat and 1 part perlite. After this has been placed in the pit, a thin covering of perlite is placed on top to increase the light intensity around the cuttings and speed up rooting.

The Cutting (earlies and lates)

Most basal shoots make good propagating material, reasonably soft and vegetative. Stem cuttings are sometimes hard and woody: these don't make good rooting material, invariably producing premature buds. Soft stem cuttings are just as good as basal growths. Break off the growths with finger and thumb, making cuttings of about 50mm (2in) long. Take off the bottom leaf and dip

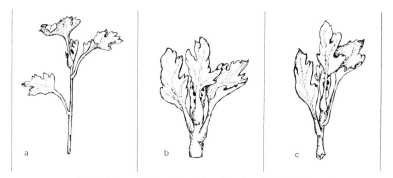

Fig 4 a) Poor, thin cutting; b) cutting too fat; c) ideal cutting

Rooting in Jiffy 7s

the end of the stem in a hormone rooting powder. Just push the cuttings into the rooting compost about 18mm (¾in) deep and water them in well with a fine-rosed can.

The pit need not be covered, providing the vents and doors are kept closed. With an air temperature of 5°C (40°F) and a soil temperature of 13° to 15°C (55° to 60°F) rooting will take place in fourteen days. If there is any premature wilting, a spray over the top will bring them back up overnight. Some growers have a thermostat fitted to the pit and set it to 21°C (70°F). I switch on manually each evening and off again in the morning, varying the times according to the prevailing temperatures.

If no electricity is available, a paraffin heater under the pit is an adequate substitute. The main essentials are an aerated compost, sufficient heat and moisture, clean material and a closed house. If there is strong sunlight on them all day in February or March, a single sheet of newspaper placed over the cuttings will keep them on course.

Quite a few growers seem to like the alternative method of rooting in Jiffy 7s, small cylindrical peat blocks about 6mm (¼in) thick. When soaked in water they expand to 37mm (1½in) tall and will take one cutting. Each plant is in its own individual container and is ready for potting on when the roots appear through the sides.

The Next Composts

When your cuttings have rooted and the roots are 12 to 25mm (½ to 1in) long, they are ready for a move into a compost such as John Innes No1. The one I use is 6 parts loam, 2 parts peat and 1 part perlite, along with 135g (4oz) of John Innes base fertiliser and 203g (6oz) of Seagold per bushel (four 2gal buckets) of mix. The John Innes recommended alternative is 8 parts sterilised loam, 2½ parts peat and 1½ parts grit, plus (per bushel) 135g (4oz) John Innes base and 25g (¾oz) calcium carbonate. The important thing here and with any future compost containing grit is that your grit must be sharp, hard, clean and about 4 or 5mm (⅛ or ₁₆³in) in particle size.

Pot Growing

There are a few ways of growing earlies from now until they go into the bed, but the two best methods are the pot and frame-base methods. I believe that growing in pots will give you superior plants, but it is rather time-consuming and they need fairly constant attention. The other way is to go from the propagating pit into tomato trays, then into the base of the cold frame, and from there into the bed.

If you decide to go the pot way, 90mm (3½in) pots are the first size you will require. I prefer clay pots to plastic. They are porous, so they breathe better and seem far more conducive to the production of a healthy vigorous root system. Pots must be clean and should be soaked in clean water and the surplus allowed to dry off before potting takes place. The compost you use should be of the correct moisture content which can be checked as follows. Take a handful of compost and squeeze it gently, then open your hand and touch the sample with your other hand – the compost should fall. If it doesn't fall it is too wet; if it falls before you touch it, it is too dry.

When both pot and compost have the correct moisture content, you are ready to lift the rooted cuttings from the pit. Fill the pot to just over halfway with compost, introduce the cutting and add

The plant on the left has been grown in a plastic pot, the other in a clay pot. Note the difference

more compost to cover the roots, which should be evenly spaced. A tap on the bench with the pot will consolidate the compost sufficiently. Leave about 12mm (½in) at the top of the pot for future watering. The plants may now be stood very close together on the bench, which should have been damped down.

If you have done the job right, the plants should not require water for about ten to fourteen days. The roots have to be encouraged to seek and find moisture, so if you water before they really require watering, you will not produce the best possible root system. Making your plant search for its moisture, and only watering when it really starts to wilt, will build up a vigorous root system and a short jointed top with a good spread. As growth increases, the plants will need spacing out, and ventilation in favourable conditions.

Potting on
From the 90mm (3½in) pots the plants should go into 125mm (5in) or 150mm (6in) pots with the same type of compost, but this time double up on the fertiliser per bushel. If you are using calcium carbonate, double up on this as well; but if you are using Seagold, keep to 203g (6oz) per bushel.

22

Pot on when the roots have grown well round the outside and look white and healthy. Don't be too impatient to do the job, but, on the other hand, don't let the plant get rootbound. Again, make sure the moisture content of compost and pot are right. Use crocks in the bottom of the pot and cover them with a few beech or oak leaves before you introduce the new compost. Push or firm this down gently with your knuckles. Water the plant, knock it out of its little pot and place it on this compost. Place more compost round the soil ball, just covering it, easing the compost gently into place using fingers and thumbs or a small potting stick – do not firm or ram too hard. Finally, make sure that the old soil ball is covered with about 12mm (½in) of compost, and that about 18mm (¾in) is left at the top for watering later on. Label and stand out in a frost-proof cold frame as soon as possible. Again, ten to fourteen days should pass before you have to water. Open up the frame lights on all favourable occasions.

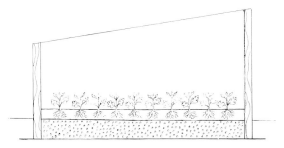

Fig 5 Section through the cold frame when earlies have been bedded out. Below ground level is 150mm (6in) of weathered ash or fine gravel. The plants are in 75mm (3in) of John Innes No 1 compost, and should be 150mm (6in) apart

The Frame-base Method

If you wish an easier ride through the early stages, go from the propagating pit into tomato trays and John Innes No1 compost. Put 20 plants in each tray and, when these are growing into each other, move them into John Innes No2 compost on the bottom of the frame. The frame should be as light as possible and deep enough to accommodate a plant ½m (20in) high at one side and a little lower at the other. The frame base should be porous: either gravel, sand or weathered ash to a depth of at least 75mm (3in) on the floor, with the same amount of compost on top. Space your

Earlies in a box before going into the frame base

plants about 150mm (6in) apart and use a board to stand on in the frame when planting. Gently firm in with your hands and, provided the gravel, sand or ash was watered well before introducing the compost, the plants should not require water for weeks. They will get sufficient moisture up through the base by capillary attraction, presuming that the lights are kept on for a few weeks, and opened only in very favourable conditions. Don't be tempted to water until the plants really ask for it, ie when they are a dull blue-green and limpness is visible in the mornings. Keep the frost out and take off the lights as much as you can in the later stages. Propping the lights up at both ends for about 150mm (6in) lets the air circulate around the plants and keeps the rain out. In some seasons the plants will require no water at all until just before leaving the frame in May.

Preparing the Early Bed

The site for a new bed should be as open as possible: full sun is a distinct advantage and provision must be made for wind protection. Some kind of overhead protection is generally considered necessary at flowering time and visits to a few growers will reveal the best type for you. The most popular protector is a timber framework similar in shape to a greenhouse. A polythene sheet (or polythene-covered frames) may be draped over or fastened to this structure, about the time of colour show. The eaves-height should be about 2m (6ft 6in) and the ridge-height

2.5m (8ft 2in). An alternative is to use metal scaffold poles or angle-iron, if you can pick some up, but the cost of new ones would be prohibitive today.

There are hundreds of different soils growing earlies and it is very difficult to recommend a cultural routine that will satisfy every soil. To generalise, double digging can be practised either in the early winter on heavy ground or in the early spring on light ground, incorporating well-rotted farmyard manure in the top of the bottom trench and up the trench side as you progress.

About fourteen days before planting out, fork into the top of the bed about 135 to 203g per sq m (4 to 6oz per sq yd) of a balanced chrysanthemum fertiliser such as Eclipse Compound Fish Manure, or 271g per sq m (8oz per sq yd) of John Innes base fertiliser.

Old beds

If your bed has grown chrysanthemums before, you can still use farmyard manure in the normal way, but the application of dressings before planting will vary according to how you have previously fed your bed and how long you have been growing on the area.

If you have been growing for a long time and flower quality is to your satisfaction, continue in the same way, but if flower quality has

Digging in farmyard manure – an essential

deteriorated it is possible that you have too much phosphate and potash in your ground. As nitrogen is generally used up or leached out of the soil every year, it may pay you to apply a pre-planting dressing consisting only of nitrogen. This can take the form of hoof and horn meal at 100g per sq m (3oz per sq yd), or Nitroform or Gold N, both slow-release nitrogenous fertilisers, at the rate of 34g per sq m (1oz per sq yd). Many of today's nationally known growers use this method.

Stopping and Timing

Half the battle in growing for show is having the flowers there on the right day. One year, the Northern Group show was held on 16 –17 September and I required 25 vases of five. For the National show, four days later, I required another 21 vases. This meant I needed a total of 46 vases inside four days, and all had to be top quality. I was placed first at Harrogate, plus best vase, and managed to win the 9 vase and 6 vase classes at London. The four-word telegram I received from a top exhibitor has stuck in my mind ever since: it summed up the whole situation with 'Congratulations on the timing'.

Too often we hear the man in the exhibition hall criticising the winning blooms with remarks like 'I had better last week', but even if he did, that is irrelevant on the day. In Yorkshire we would say, 'Put up or shut up'.

The majority of earlies grown for exhibition are on what is known as first crown. The growing point is removed on a certain date and the resulting laterals produce the flowers. If the plant is in a vegetative state of growth, remove as little as possible, but make sure that the stem is completely severed and you have not just taken the top leaves. If the plant is nearing the natural break, that is just making a bud, you must go further down the plant and take up (grow on) the sixth or seventh lateral.

Dates for stopping the various cultivars may be found in the Northern Group's *Stopping Times* (see page 61) and raisers' catalogues.

The weather can influence flowering dates, so, for example, if a cultivar's stopping date is 10 May and you have grown a dozen plants, stop four a week before, four on 10 May and four the week after. This way you should be able to have a cut on your show day.

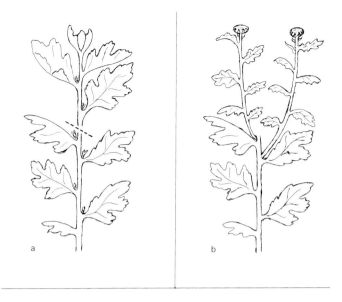

Fig 6 a) When the plant is nearing its natural break, cut off the break bud and the first five laterals; b) resultant laterals after a hard stop

Break-bud flowering

Another way, especially with intermediates, is to root your cuttings later, some time in March, and grow them without stopping, allowing the break bud to develop into the flower. You have to grow about ten of a cultivar to make fairly sure of a vase and if you root some ten days earlier and some ten days later, that makes thirty, but you can plant much closer together.

Second-crown flowering

Not many earlies come really good this way, but sometimes a cultivar responds well. Stop once and then stop the resultant laterals again to give second-crown blooms. This gives a later bloom and probably better colour but in all probability the blooms will possess fewer florets. These factors can be used to advantage with certain cultivars.

Run-on flowering

If a first-crown plant produces its bud too early you can take the next lateral down from the bud and hope it produces a flower of quality. It doesn't often come good but this run-on principle occasionally works.

Planting Out

The pot-grown earlies will determine their own time to go out into the bed. A healthy white vigorous root system over the outside of the soil ball tells you that it is time for a move, but if the roots become matted it is getting too late. So, obviously, the bed must be ready and the weather must be favourable at the same time. Soil temperature must be about 10°C (50°F) in the early part of the day, and the soil must be dry enough to walk on without it sticking to your shoes. The weather should be fairly settled. To create these conditions, you may have to put on your overhead covers beforehand to warm up the soil or keep it fairly dry. Rokolene netting around the bed will keep out a gale force wind. I plant out between the third week in April and the third week in May, depending on the state of the plants and the weather.

If your plants are being grown in the frame base, far more latitude can be given, for they will stay there happily, without spoiling, up to a couple of weeks more than the pot-grown ones before planting out.

Method
Fork and rake over the bed to obtain a fine tilth, run out a line and insert canes at your planting distance. Mine is 450mm (1ft 6in); my rows are the same distance apart, with three rows to a bed and a path of 760mm (2ft 6in) between beds. If the bed is at all sticky, use boards to walk on.

Using a spade, dig out holes up to the canes, deep enough to take the soil balls of the potted plants (or the depth of the frame compost) plus 50mm (2in). Both pot and frame plants should have been watered the day before you plant. Knock the plants out of the pots (or lift them from the frame with a hand fork) and place them in the holes. Introduce soil around the balls, firm them in with your hands and make sure that they are covered with about 25mm (1in) of soil. Leave a saucer-shaped depression around each plant about 25mm (1in) deep, for future watering, if needed.

Tie the plants to your canes, or use wire rings. Protect them (with Rokolene netting) from the gales which generally threaten at this time of year. Don't be tempted to water them or they will become lazy. Let them search for their moisture, only watering if they flag badly in the morning.

Overhead spraying of earlies in hot weather

Overhead Spraying

The general tendency is to reach for the fertiliser bag when your plants are growing well, though this is probably the worst thing you can do. It is far better to let them build up a good root system, encouraging growth in really hot weather by overhead spraying. Use the fine rose on your hose pipe or can to wet the foliage (but not the bed), then allow the water to evaporate. I have repeated this process anything up to six times a day in hot weather before the buds appear. If you are not at home during the day, you will need a willing helper.

Thinning Down and Side Shoots

When the laterals are long enough to fasten to individual canes, they can be thinned down, leaving two on large cultivars and three per plant on mediums. This encourages larger blooms. Cut them off, don't be tempted to tear or rip. Some cultivars can have an extra lateral left on to keep petal count down. It is removed when

29

the buds begin to swell, to keep the size up to the potential for the cultivar. Ginger Nut responds well to this treatment.

Side shoots will appear in the leaf axils as the breaks elongate. These must be taken off as soon as possible.

Nitrogen

Do not be tempted to give extra nitrogenous feeds or your plant will be soft and lush and the resultant flowers will be of poor quality. Ripe, firm wood is required, with reddish rather than green stems, which should feel firm when tested about 200mm (8in) from the top. Soft, unripe stems are easily created and, once in that condition, are most difficult to ripen. Too much nitrogen makes the leaves too deep a green, so keep an eye on them. A mid green (eg privet) is the colour to aim for.

Bud Initiation and Securing

Late June will probably herald bud initiation. If you are growing on a newish bed, a light dressing of a chrysanthemum fertiliser at the rate of 68g per sq m (2oz per sq yd), hoed and watered in, should see your plants through to the end. Old beds should not require this dressing. In July, the buds will appear, and they must be secured when the surrounding side shoots are about 12mm (½in) long. These small laterals which come around the centre buds have to be nipped or levered off.

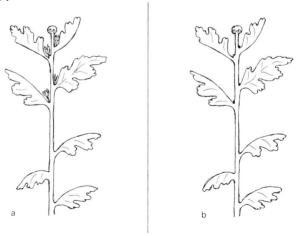

Fig 7 a) Bud before securing, with sideshoots; b) after securing

Some cultivars, such as Venice, have to be secured when the laterals are very small, otherwise the main bud aborts and is lost. Others, such as Cornish, will be quite happy with side shoots 25mm (1in) long. Some growers refer to this process as 'taking the bud', though we actually leave it on and secure it. The bud will become a flower in seven to nine weeks' time. Make sure the plants are kept watered at this stage and at all times afterwards – water below and not overhead.

Covers and Bud-bags

Most early exhibitors have some form of metal or wood structure surrounding their bed so that polythene-covered or glass frames may be fixed over the plants. Generally, the covers go on when colour begins to show on the buds. Don't put them on too soon, or the necks of those not showing colour will tend to elongate.

Bud-bags and bloom-bags (behind). The cut-out bag shows the position of the bud

If you have early buds and don't want to put the covers on too soon, bag them with a double bud-bag 150mm (6in) square, fastened with a paper/wire tie. This will keep the rain off and the insects out. Do this when the calyx splits, changing to the larger bags when floret length is about 25mm (1in). It is often useful to use bud-bags on the colours (as well as the usual whites and yellows) for about the first ten days after calyx split. Cover the side ends of the structure with Rokolene netting, which allows the air to circulate. It need not come down to ground level – just below bloom level will suffice.

Bagging

An early bed in an exhibitor's garden is no lovely sight at this time of the year, for greaseproof bloom-bags seem to be the predominant sight. Bloom-bags are used on whites, yellows, pale pinks and some light bronzes; never on reds, purples, pinks and bronzes or they will take out most of the colour. They are used on incurves, intermediates and certain reflexes. They broaden and elongate florets, and make blooms a little larger. They also help the loose 'skirty' intermediates by keeping up the lower florets and improving the form of the bloom. Cultivars like Cornish benefit from this treatment.

The usual bag sizes are 250 x 250mm (10 x 10in) for medium cultivars and 300 x 325mm (12 x 13in) for large. The smaller bag may sometimes be used for large incurves, like Winnie Bramley and Eda Fitton, if it has been fitted correctly. Single bags may be used under covers, but, if no covers are available, double bags are the best. Place the bags in a damp atmosphere (eg under the covers at ground level) before putting them on. They will then be pliable and easy to mould to the necks.

To fit a bag, gather the neck neatly, hold between forefinger and thumb, and make a finger-sized hole in the open end. Inflate it like a balloon. Place the bag over the bud (whose neck should be stiff enough to support it), mould neatly around the stem and fasten with a paper/wire tie. Support the bag with one hand and press down on the top to position the bag around the bud. You should feel a resistance from the air pressure inside. Put the date on each

Author adjusting bags on earlies. Note the netting folded up at the top of the picture

N.C.S. Silver Medal to
Best Vase in Show

bag. All cultivars with the same date on will be ready at the same time. Check whether they are ready by looking into one bag. They are generally ready after three to four weeks in the bags. Be very careful when removing the bags. Tear open the tops and take them off without bruising the florets. A friend of mine once said that opening a bag was more exciting than courting!

Temperature Control

Some sort of shading will be a necessity in hot sunny weather, for high temperatures under covers cause loss of colour. I like to use Coolglass, a white shading paste, under my glass top-light covers. This allows plenty of light through, but keeps the sun from scorching the opening blooms and reduces the temperature around the blooms. The stronger colours (eg Formcast, Red Formcast and other purples, reds and deep bronzes) can be kept cooler by growing them behind a hessian screen on one side of the structure, instead of the Rokolene netting. Fans may be used to move the air under the covers. With large structures, an aperture can be left at the top to let the hot air out, but an extra polythene ridge will have to be placed about 75mm (3in) above the aperture to keep out the rain.

(*top*) This vase of Sam Vinter won an NCS silver medal for best vase in show at the Northern Group Show, Harrogate, 1979

(*below*) This vase of Pink Gin, a late spray, won best vase in show at Harrogate, 1980

4 Growing Lates

Late growing is totally different to early growing, for lates spend the majority of their life with a restricted root system in the confines of a plant pot. This has the advantage that they grow in fresh new compost each year without the build-up of nutrients which can so easily happen in early beds.

The late man's year starts during late October or November before flowering takes place. New basal growth is cut down to a leaf joint above soil level, and the resultant shoots will develop ready for taking in during the Christmas period or the New Year. My approximate date for this operation is about eight to ten weeks before I require the cuttings. The new material from the base is excellent for propagation.

Fig 8 Late stool with basal growths cut off. Cuttings will come a few weeks later

When stock selection has been carried out as with the earlies (see page 15), subject the greenhouse to low temperatures. After the last show in November I turn my heat off and give just frost protection. This gives the stools a type of vernalisation which is considered a necessity for lates.

36

I prefer to leave the old stools in their pots; but they can be taken out, cut into a 150mm (6in) square and boxed; or shaken out and treated as the earlies (see page 17). Any that are required early can be given a little bottom heat by standing them on a cable or heating pipes.

Propagating

Large exhibition cultivars such as Pink Duke and the Gigantic sports are generally put to root about late December to late January, followed by the other types in February and early March. One cannot be dogmatic about rooting dates – again *Stopping Times* (see page 61) and catalogues are the best help, along with a knowledge of a cultivar's natural flowering time. Treat them the same as earlies at this stage (see page 18). From the rooting pit, move them into small pots and then into 125mm (5in) pots, or (for those with more vigorous roots) 150mm (6in) pots. Again, I prefer clay pots, but plastic can still do a good job.

I use the same composts as for the earlies (see page 19) but, if soil is out of the question, I would use 3 parts granulated sphagnum peat and 1 part grit or perlite, plus a Chempak no-soil additive, which has full instructions on the bag. One Chempak bag makes 2 bushels (16gal) of ready-to-use compost for all size pottings.

Put the plants out into the frame as soon as possible and water only when they really flag. Keep the frost out by using carpets, felt or even straw to cover the lights when frost threatens. Listen carefully to your regional weather forecast right through to April and May. Cane each plant in the frame, fastening it with a ring, for some of them grow quite tall. Watch for aphids – spray or drench as soon as one is seen. Ventilate as much as possible when the weather is favourable.

Stopping and Timing

Generally speaking, the rules for stopping and timing are the same as for earlies (see page 26). The majority of lates, such as Mark Woolman and Fair Lady, are grown on first-crown buds, with a few on second. Second-crown growing is used to obtain a later flower and reduce petal count. This is useful for some cultivars which have too many florets on early buds. Edith Woolman, Sam Vinter, Purple Glow and Silver Ley respond to second-crown treatment.

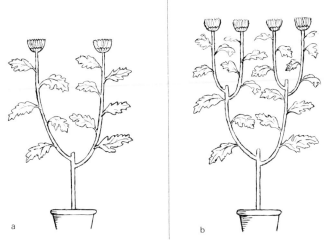

Fig 9 a) First-crown buds after a stop or pinch; b) second-crown buds after two stops

Stopping twice delays bud initiation, and when a bud develops in shortening days it has fewer florets and develops much faster than one forming in long days. If the flower is an incurved, the top will close over without the lower florets becoming old and soft. Bill Florentine, Shirley Olympic and Heather James respond to this treatment. Singles are often grown this way, then cropped well so that the rows of florets are not too numerous – refinement is the order of the day. Annina, Woolman's Glory and their sports are better grown like this. A later-developing bud will also give a better-coloured flower because it is forming in lower temperatures.

Alternative methods
Break-bud growing is a possibility with lates which is not often practised nowadays. Large exhibitions rooted in May and flowered one up in 150mm (6in) pots were quite common a few years ago, and still offer an interesting challenge to the exhibitor.

Good blooms with excellent colour and form are sometimes seen from run-on buds. Generally the bud has come too soon and the next lateral down has been run on.

Sometimes a cultivar is recommended to be grown on a natural break. In this case the plant is not stopped and a break bud will appear in the growing point. Then go down the stem if it is a large exhibition and grow up for example the sixth or seventh lateral for your flower. Laterals six, seven and eight would be grown on for your flowers in the case of incurved, reflexed or intermediates. A

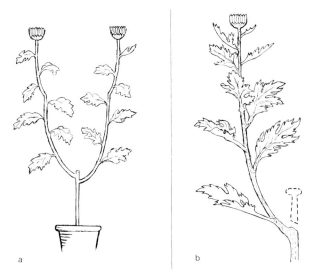

Fig 10 a) Run-on buds when first-crown buds came too early; b) run-on bud, showing where first-crown bud has been rubbed off

natural second will be one of these laterals producing a bud again and the resultant breaks being taken up to produce the blooms.

From these remarks you can see that there are dozens of different ways to produce a flower. Before you decide which one to use, think about the cultivar, the show date, the floret count, the form and the colour. Remember also that some cultivars produce blooms with insufficient florets if their buds are secured in short days – the result is a daisy eye. Shirley Model, Fairweather and all their sports show these symptoms if buds are secured too late.

Composts for Final Potting

Prepare and mix your compost about two to three weeks before it is required in May or June. I like my final mixes to be of a similar physical structure to the ones used in the other pottings. I use 6 parts loam, 2 parts peat and 1 part perlite, plus the following to each bushel: 305g (9oz) of Bentley's No1 chrysanthemum fertiliser, 170g (5oz) bonemeal, 203g (6oz) Seagold, 68g (2oz) magnesium sulphate (epsom salts) and sufficient ground chalk to bring the pH up to 6.5.

When I was using very hard bore-hole water, I found that lime in the form of calcium carbonate was completely unnecessary in the composts. But now I have a soft water supply, I test for lime or calcium when mixing the composts, using a Rapitest pH soil-test kit, which is a very reliable meter. This year I had to use 102g (3oz) of ground chalk per bushel to bring the pH to 6.5.

I have also used the John Innes mix of 8 parts loam, 2½ parts peat and 1½ parts Shap granite, plus the same fertiliser addition as above. In both mixes the loam should be sterilised to keep weeds down in the final pots. This makes the plants a little heavier after potting on, as sterilisation adds extra nitrogen.

Pass all the loam and peat through a 16mm (⅝in) riddle before mixing, and turn the whole mixture about six times, keeping an eye on the moisture content (see page 21). It can be stored in polythene bags or kept, covered, on a concrete floor to keep the moisture in.

I always remember asking a famous grower of large exhibitions what was the most important facet of their culture, in his eyes. He inferred that most growers did not realise the importance of grit in their composts. Your potting composts should be free draining, making it impossible for them to get waterlogged, so it is of paramount importance that the right type of grit or perlite is used. If your loam is very fine or on the clay side of heavy, it pays to increase the amount of grit or perlite in your compost. I would never accept a compost that still showed water on the top of the soil ball longer than a minute after watering.

I use 216mm (8½in) or 228mm (9in) or 254mm (10in) clay pots, but it is possible to use plastic, especially if you are using the same no-soil mix as given above. Wash and scrub clean the pots (and the crocks) after soaking them in a bath of clear water. Obtain a good supply of dry beech or oak leaves from the previous year's fall (to help drainage). Then wait until the root system is well round the outside of the balls in the small pots. When you can see more root than compost they are ready for the move. Water them the night before potting.

Final Potting

About 5 May the first of the large exhibitions should be in the final pots, with the other types following on when ready. Remember, this is purely dependent on the prevailing weather conditions and root systems. The larger pots take the vigorously rooted plants like Duke of Kent and Jessie Habgood; the smaller sizes are for those

Lates stood 'pot thick' after final potting

with less prolific root systems like Peggy Ann and Leviathan and incurves and singles.

Soak the pots again on the morning of potting and allow the surplus to dry off. Put in the crocks and cover with leaves – ideal drainage. Add the compost and firm gently with your knuckles. Remove the pot from the young plant, take out the crocks and introduce the plant to its new home. It should be positioned so that,

Fig 11 Section through final pot, showing beech or oak leaves above the crocks, to help drainage

when covered with 25mm (1in) of compost, there is still about 50mm (2in) of space for top dressings and waterings. Add more compost, firm down the sides with your fingers and level off.

With these composts a very hard firming is not required, but firm in more on the incurved and intermediates. Stand the plants outside, pot thick, for about three weeks. Water only when they really ask for it. Spray overhead when the sun is hot, and be prepared to cover against frost and heavy rain if they come (see page 41).

Whilst the plants are pot thick you will probably come across the larvae of the codling moth in some growing points. It will seal the points over and eat out the growing tip unless you hand pick the small, brown, caterpillar-like grub as soon as it starts work. I have found no sprays that are 100 per cent effective in keeping them away.

Lining Out and Caning

After the period of standing out pot thick, line the plants out on wooden battens about 37mm (1½in) apart, in 6m (20ft) rows, with rows just less than 1m (3ft) apart. Place supporting posts at either end of the row with galvanised wire stretched between them, the wire height being determined by the height potential of the plant.

Fig 12 Lates stood out on wooden battens

Generally, with large exhibitions, such as Harry Gee and Shirley Primrose, two canes are inserted to support the growing plants, which are fastened to the wire with metal clips. With other types, such as Sam Vinter and Fairweather, three or four canes are used. When pushing the canes in, try to keep them away from the inner soil ball. Fasten breaks to the canes as soon as they can be safely fastened without tearing the lateral from the main stem.

Number of laterals

To encourage large blooms, large exhibitions are generally grown with two laterals up to the bud and then reduced to one. I like to grow incurves with five or six laterals up to the bud, then reduce to four or five and sometimes down to three final laterals on housing. Decoratives should have four or five laterals, reduced to three, with no less than two laterals on certain cultivars.

Large singles can be grown with seven to nine laterals, reducing to six in mid August; medium singles may carry eight to fourteen flowering laterals, depending on the petal count of the cultivar. Get to know your cultivars and work accordingly: if the petal count of your flowers is too high, increase the number of blooms to reduce it next year.

When reducing the number of laterals, growers often cut the top few inches off the first day, and wait a couple of days between each further cut, until the whole lateral has been removed.

By growing more laterals than you are going to flower, before the bud is seen, root production is encouraged. Then, by cutting off one lateral a little bit at a time, the sap flow is gradually directed to the remaining lateral or laterals, thus producing a larger flower or flowers in November. With incurved cultivars, such as Fairweather, better form is obtained by cutting off the weakest of the remaining four laterals (well budded by this time) when housing in late September. This reduces the ultimate petal count, but the root system that supported the original five laterals is now directed into producing three flowers which will have better form and size.

Watering

If you grow a chrysanthemum in dry conditions right through the season you will have hard, brittle and very ripe wood and the resultant flowers will be small. Similarly, if you grow in wet conditions all the time, you will have soft, lush unripe wood, a gross

Watering lates

plant and, again, poor, small flowers or flowers on top. Aim to alternate between wetness and dryness, lushness and hardness, controlling the type of wood you grow by correct use of the watering can. Moisture plays a very important part in the production of an exhibition bloom.

Method
My watering routine is generally carried out before early evening, and preferably in the mornings. I use a pot tapper, a length of cane with a cylindrical block of hardwood about the size of a cotton reel on the end. I tap the pots about halfway up and water only if they ring with a bell-like tone. If there is no ring, just a dullish tone, I do not water – it is as simple as that. A 10l (2gal) can will water about ten plants.

If you are growing in a no-soil compost or using plastic pots, another technique will have to be mastered. The dryness of the compost's surface or the dull appearance of the growing point will indicate when it is time to apply the water. The 'campanology' technique will not work either if you have got cracked pots, though they can be repaired quite easily by breaking them apart and fixing with Araldite.

Feeding

The main aim is to get a large, firm, ripe-wooded plant with leaves not too deep a green in colour. This can be achieved by using a balanced chrysanthemum fertiliser at the manufacturer's recommended rates of application. I use Bentley's No1 chrysanthemum fertiliser at the rate of 1 level teaspoonful per plant or even down to half that amount on some cultivars, such as Shirley Champion and Sam Vinter, never more. Apply it once a week and water it in, making sure that plants are moist before any feed is given. Never feed a dry plant.

More blooms are ruined by overfeeding than anything else, so don't be tempted to heap the spoon, and don't be in too much of a hurry to start. Wait for at least six weeks after final potting, slightly less on no-soil composts.

Two top dressings of final compost mix can be given about mid July and mid August – about 6mm (¼in) each time. Just before the buds appear, one liquid feed may be given in between the solid feeds. Use something with a balanced analysis, eg the 20/20/20 ratio of Chempak No3.

After the bud
When the bud appears, it is advisable to increase the amount of nitrogen in the feed so I change to Bentley's No2 fertiliser, at the same rate as above. Stop feeding as soon as the calyx splits, even before this with soft-petalled cultivars such as Arnold Fitton and Fair Lady.

Keep the side shoots down and secure the buds in just the same way as for earlies (see page 31). Observe all the plant-health routines (see Chapter 6), keep the basal growth pruned down and remove any dead or damaged leaves at the base of the plants.

Bud-bags may be used when the calyx splits on the earliest buds. It often pays to leave them out of the greenhouse for as long as you can so as to ripen and firm the necks.

A liquid alternative

If you prefer to use liquid feeds all the way through, the Chempak range is ideal. I have grown many good flowers by this method. Start off with Chempak No4 and alternate with Chempak No3 (sometimes I mix them, according to the weather pattern and the look of the plant), then finish with No2 and No3 mixed, stopping the feeding before colour shows. The advantage of using the Chempak liquid fertilisers is that they contain seven invaluable trace elements. Don't be tempted to use more than the stated amounts.

If at any time during July and August the foliage looks pale or chloritic, apply Murphy Plant Tonic or Sequestrene at the recommended strengths – generally only twice per season.

Feeding Routines

It is important to keep the same cultural routine for the whole season. Don't start off with, for instance, a soil compost in clay pots and then change over to a no-soil compost for final potting. Decide what feed you are going to use and try to stick to that, changing only when weather patterns and quality of wood suggest a different analysis. So often, I have seen a new grower ruin his plants because someone has come along and told him to use something different. Advice is taken, and before you realise what has happened, your plants are really out of balance and condition, and the flowers are ruined.

There is no secret feed that comes out of the waistcoat pocket when no one is around – nothing could be further from the truth! I once grew eight rows of lates with each row on a different feed right through the season (all recommended chrysanthemum feeds, some liquid and some solid organics). At the end of the day, all the rows gave me similar flowers. Yet different growers using the same feed each week at the same time would all finish up with totally different blooms. It is not exactly which feed you use that really counts, but all the other points of culture.

Some growers will advise you to feed your blooms instead of your plants, others will say the opposite. You have to sort it all out in your own way. I believe there are two different ways of producing good flowers. The first produces a really firm, ripe plant, not too big, with a light-green leaf. This can be obtained by keeping down the feed and using one with more potash than nitrogen up to bud securing. Then change over to a feed with a little more nitrogen after bud securing, stopping when the calyx splits. Start bloom feeding when the flowers are about one-third out, using a liquid feed at normal strength, one with a nitrogen emphasis. Two feeds with a week or ten days between should do the job. Don't be tempted to go on too long or give too much, or there is a chance of ruining your flowers. Remember, this method can only be practised if the plant is in the right condition.

The second way is to produce a very large, firm, ripe plant (as we have discussed in this chapter) and stop feeding at or just before calyx split. Then allow the flower to develop by just using water. There are sufficient nutrients in the pot to see the bloom through to the show bench, provided that normal feeding routines have been practised.

You decide which way you are going to grow and stick to it.

Overfeeding
If things have not worked out too well for you over the years and your flowers are not up to top quality, ask yourself if your feeding routine is too heavy. More cherished flowers are ruined by too rich a diet than by a poor one. I know that chrysanthemums are gross feeders, but having talked to growers of both earlies and lates and seen their substandard blooms, I found that their plants were receiving far more nutrients than mine. If excess food is given early, your plants become too good, too soon. I like them to improve gradually, so that the climax of growth is reached on the day I cut the flower. It does not always happen like that, but that is the theory. Have the courage to reduce the feeding if necessary, and note the effect.

Into the Greenhouse

By mid to late September, the greenhouse should have been thoroughly cleaned down, washed out and ventilated. The lates can come in when colour is showing on the buds. Spray them with insecticide and fungicide before they go in, and stand them fairly close, but not so close that the blooms will touch when developed. Keep all vents fully open (I even have them in the brick walls round the base), and gradually colour will fill your greenhouse.

Lates in the greenhouse, fairly close together, with tubular heaters overhead

Humidity and air circulation

When the petals really start to lengthen from early October onwards, the outside air gradually becomes moist and the nights are still and damp. A little warmth is necessary to make the atmosphere drier and circulate the air. I recommend tubular heaters, placed about 300mm (1ft) above the blooms, and these are switched on manually when the air outside is stagnant. Keep the top vents closed (after the sun has gone down or early evening) but all bottom vents open to maintain a dry atmosphere around the flowers. Use a couple of oscillating fans to move the air gently around the blooms. This will virtually eliminate the menace of damping. Close the door in the early evening during this period and open it in the morning if it is fine.

If you have pipes round the base of the greenhouse (or a paraffin heater), the top vents should be left slightly open to move the air around. Whichever method you use, a fan to circulate the air is a distinct advantage.

Water little and often, mornings only.

5 Other Types

Sprays

A spray is either the last flowering growth or lateral, emerging from the last stop or natural break (early sprays are grown this way for exhibition); or the main stem of a short-season plant, which produces no laterals, but develops blooms on pedicels emerging from its main (terminal) stem (late sprays are grown this way for exhibition).

The terminal spray with only one bloom on a pedicel is regarded as the perfect spray form. If a terminal spray has compounded, with more than one bloom on a pedicel, secondary blooms (or buds) on sub-pedicels should be removed. If the secondary buds or blooms are not removed, it will have to be shown in a class for compound sprays.

Early sprays
Treat these the same as earlies, but root about mid March, box into tomato trays twelve plants to the box, go into the frame and out into the bed mid May, and stop towards the end of May. Allow the

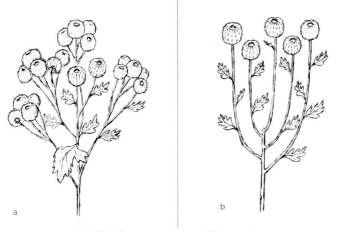

Fig 13 a) Compound spray; b) terminal spray

Other Types

plants to grow freely and leave all breaks on, thinning down in late June to four breaks per plant. Use netting as a support to save all caning and tying. When the buds appear and are about pea size, remove the centre bud of each stem and limit the other buds on that stem to the most even five, six, seven or eight. Then wait for the blaze of colour from these fantastic weatherproof flowers. There is no need for covers. Good exhibition sprays are: Margaret P and sports, Pennine Wine DR, Marion PY, Yellow Heide Y and Apricot Madeleine LB.

Late sprays
These are a different kettle of fish – requiring only four months' growing time from rooting in early July to putting on the show bench in November. They are best rooted in Jiffy 7s in a closed frame, then moved into 127mm (5in) pots using John Innes No2 compost. Growth will be fast. As soon as roots are round the outside, move into 215mm (8½in) pots or butcher's liver containers (1gal), with drainage holes drilled in their bases. Use the same mix. They can be grown outside or inside.

I find the easiest way to get propagating material in early July, of the right size and thickness, is to put cuttings from the old stools to root in February. When rooted, box up like earlies about twelve to a tray, using John Innes No1 compost. Then cut them down in the boxes to 100mm (4in) high, about four weeks before the cuttings are required. Give a liquid feed of Chempak No2 to the boxes of small cut-off plants, and you will be rewarded with plenty of good vegetative cutting material in early July. This saves looking after the old stools, with their fast, tangled growth and substandard cuttings.

Seventy days before your show, black them out for thirteen hours a night with dense black polythene. Mine goes on at 18.00hr and comes off at 07.00hr. Do this for a period of three weeks – the difference it makes to the finished product is unbelievable. Buds

(*top*) Part of a display of Large Exhibition blooms at the NCS National Show, Westminster, 1982. Back row (left to right): Lilac Prince, Cream Duke, Leviathan, Ruby Edwards, Leviathan. Centre row: Cream Duke, Lilac Prince, Jessie Habgood, Silver Gigantic. Front row: Elizabeth Shoesmith, Fred Taylor, Gigantic, Pink Shoesmith, Golden Gigantic

(*below*) Three vases of earlies: Yellow Margaret Riley, Margaret Riley and Salmon Margaret Riley. This exhibit won a silver medal in the North of England Championship class, Doncaster, 1980

are initiated all the way down the plant, and they all flower at the same time. A good late spray should have about twenty flowers, each on a pedicel coming from a leaf joint on the main stem. Give the plants an occasional liquid feed, and remove each spray's centre bud when pea size. Late sprays do not need stopping. To time the flowers, use your rooting date and blacking-out time. Almost fifty days after blacking out they should be on the show bench. Try to keep the temperature between 10° and 15°C (50° to 60°F).

Transporting
Taking these flowers to a show is often quite a challenge, as carrying boxes have to be enormous. Laying them down gently on the car seat or floor will get them there in a satisfactory condition.

If, when you arrive in the hall, you find that the foliage has gone limp, give the stem ends a two-minute spell in boiling water, followed by plunging into cold deep water. Similar action can revive other types of chrysanthemums, and many an exhibitor's kit includes a gas stove!

Good late exhibition sprays are: Romark W, Robeam Y, Pink Gin LPu, Roscene W, Rynoon LP, Ryflame B and Rytang B.

Specimen Plants

Specimen plants are normal, late exhibition cultivars grown in a symmetrical form with as many flowers per plant as possible. In fact I have seen single plants of Golden Princess Anne with over four hundred flowers. Not all cultivars respond to this type of culture, but excellent specimens may be grown from the cultivar Princess Anne and sports, or some of the singles like My Love.

Rooting is best in late November or early December and cuttings should be potted on as other lates, with an extra final pot, usually a 450mm (18in). About six weeks is usual between each potting.

Specimen plants require stopping four times. Four breaks are taken up at the end of January, and when these are 150mm (6in) long they are stopped again. The third stop is about the end of June and the fourth in mid July and no later.

Staking must be very methodical – about eighteen 1m (3ft)

Best Large or Medium Exhibition bloom (Jimmy Mottram) at the Northern Group Show, Harrogate, 1981

canes will eventually be required for a good plant. Never allow plants to dry out, and feed them on a regular basis from late June onwards. They will take at least twice as much feed as a normal late. Disbud the final breaks, and watch for pests and diseases. Take the plants inside in mid September, having half turned them nearly every day since they went into final pots.

If you have made a good job, you will need to widen your greenhouse door and hire a removal van to take your plant to the exhibition hall.

Charms

Charms are very decorative and most late shows have a class for them. There is probably no other plant which produces as many flowers in one season. As growth proceeds, the plant will throw out secondary shoots from its base, until it becomes a mass of wiry shoots, each of which finally terminates in a group of flower buds.

Charms can be grown from cuttings rooted in mid February and taken through the various pot sizes, to finish in a small, medium or a large one, depending on the size of plant you want. Use split canes to support the plants, and, with good cultural routines and one stop when 150mm (6in) high, you should be able to grow plants a metre across, each with two to three thousand blooms forming a symmetrical dome. Really eye catching! Don't forget to keep half turning your plants, so that a really symmetrical shape is obtained.

6 Keeping Your Plants Healthy

Probably the worst possible thing is for an insect pest eg aphids to become established in the growing points of your plants. Leaves will be distorted, the plant will be crippled, but, worst of all, there is a danger of the plant becoming infected with one of the many viruses which are passed on by sucking insects. It is of paramount importance to spray or drench regularly.

There are many types of spraying apparatus available to the grower, my own personal favourite being the foot-pump type or the compressed-air types. For systemic-insecticide application, a watering can fitted with a fine rose is ideal. Applied as an overhead drench, it is quick and effective. Don't spray in hot sunshine or wind (to avoid drift). Make sure that the plants are turgid, not dry at the roots. Wear protective clothing and rubber gloves. When you have finished, have a shower or bath and put your clothes in the wash.

With normal contact insecticides such as nicotine, malathion and Pirimor, alternate your sprays at ten or fourteen day intervals to keep on top of the enemy. With systemics such as Tumblebug or Abol G, the interval between applications may be longer.

Follow the manufacturer's instructions strictly and never, ever exceed the dose – in fact, some systemics can be used at half-strength with just the same effect. Apply them after sunset or early in the morning. I prefer the latter – there is such peace and solitude among the plants at 5.30 on a summer's morning.

Pests and Diseases

Aphids and capsid bugs are probably the worst enemies. Spray or drench as soon as you see them, or before as a preventative. If you use a nicotine spray make sure the temperature is over 16°C (60°F). Not far behind comes the earwig, which often lives in the cane ends and comes out at dusk for its meal. Catch them at that

Powdery mildew on chrysanthemum leaves

time (when they are just putting their nippers out of the top of the cane) by pushing a thick piece of wire up and down in the end of the cane. Caterpillars often cause quite a bit of damage, but Fentro will take care of them. Leaf miners make a mess of foliage, but can be controlled by a leaf-miner spray or a systemic insecticide.

Powdery mildew will often rear its ugly head in July, as a powdery white fungus on both upper and lower surfaces of the leaves. Nimrod T or Benlate, both systemic fungicides, will eradicate the menace and stop it appearing. I recommend a couple of drenches: one in early July and one in early August.

Don't worry about any of the other diseases, which only occur spasmodically. If any plant is suspect, dig it out (or take it out of its pot) and burn or destroy it; don't put it on the compost heap.

One fairly new disease is Chrysanthemum White Rust, which is now appearing in the UK. I have never seen it and don't want to, but we must all look out for it. If you see it, take off the infected leaf, or leaves, seal in a polythene bag and send it to the Ministry of Agriculture, Fisheries and Food, Diagnosis Section, Plant Pathology Laboratory, Hatching Green, Harpenden, Herts. It is first seen as pale greenish-yellow leaf spots, up to 4mm (⅛in) in diameter. On the under surface of these spots, prominent pinkish-buff pustules (raised cushion-like bodies) eventually develop. Under favourable conditions the pustules have a whitish coating, from which the disease gets its name. Here's hoping you and I never have to trouble the ministry, or have our stock devastated.

7 Showing Earlies and Lates

Before Cutting

Keep a careful watch when colour predominates. Bags on the earlies have to be straightened if they get dislodged by wind or rain, and must not rub against other blooms without bags. Watch for earwigs. Don't let the plants get dry, but, as colour really develops, don't water in the evening or the atmosphere could be too damp and spotting may occur. This applies to both earlies in the bed or lates in the greenhouse.

Reflexed flowers not in bags can be tidied up as they develop, but be very careful you do not bruise or mark any florets. Using a small (number 8) brush, a cotton-wool bud, or your finger and thumb, ease any florets which are way out of line back into a symmetrical formation, or even reflex them if they are incurving. Go round your flowers as much as you can and you will see their faults and good points. Remove cleanly any marked florets as soon as they are observed.

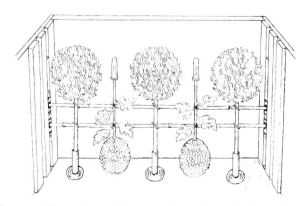

Fig 14 Large exhibition chrysanthemums fastened to a hurdle in their travelling box, with two incurved chrysanthemums upside-down between them. The test-tube and teat arrangement enables them to remain in water throughout the journey

Cutting

Never cut a bloom unless it is ready for the show bench. Once you start cutting early, you will tend to cut early each week, if you are exhibiting at quite a few shows. Remember the guidelines for a good bloom: breadth and depth in equal proportion or a globular outline. Aim at these shapes and you will be among the cards. Reflexed blooms should have a centre circular button of florets still to develop. Intermediate blooms may have a similar slight lack of development in the form of a depression on the crown of the flower, but incurved blooms should be developed to the last petal, perfectly smooth and spherical.

Some cultivars with bags on may benefit from the removal of the bag a couple of days before the show; others with skirty bases could stay on until you travel.

When you have selected the possible candidates for the show, take your vase or deep bucket of water to the plant and cut a stem about 710mm (28in) long. Strip the bottom leaves off, make a short cut vertically up the stem and plunge it straight into the water. Take the blooms into a cool garage or room and allow them to soak for twenty-four hours before moving off to the show.

Transporting

The method of transportation depends on your vehicle. Probably the safest is the hurdle box, made to fit the vehicle. Construct a box from thin waterproof plywood on light battens, and fit it with dowelling rods that slide up and down inside. The blooms are fastened on to the rods with paper/wire ties. Roughen one side of each rod with a rasp so that the blooms will not move (see Fig 14).

For long journeys, use small tubes to keep the blooms in water. I push a baby's feeding-bottle teat (narrow neck) over the stem, then put the stem into a 100 x 15mm (4 x ⅝in) test tube filled with water, and slip the teat over the neck of the tube, making a waterproof seal. If space is limited, the incurves or intermediates can be fastened on upside-down with their stems between the heads of the reflexes.

An alternative is to transport in water-filled drums with the blooms fastened to the sides; the water keeps the drums steady and upright. My other method is to carry the blooms in metal vases with large flat bases – weighted down with a couple of bricks (on a flat carpeted floor), they never move.

In other words, transport the blooms any way you like provided they don't touch or rub. Do not be tempted to use tissue paper to protect them, though with some reflexes that tend to fleck their florets, a fine hairnet is often put over the bloom.

Cutting and Transporting Large Exhibitions

When cutting these, strip the leaves off the top part of the plant first, then cut your flower (making sure you support the heavy head) and hold it upside-down. Then fix on with paper/wire ties a cane support and a wire jap ring (obtainable from Joseph Bentley, Barrow-on-Humber, Lincs). I use different-sized rings for different cultivars. Generally the incurving types are fitted with a very small ring so as not to spoil the shape, whilst the reflexed are fitted with a 50 or 75mm (2 or 3in) ring for better support. Turn the right way up, cut a piece off the end of the stem and place the blooms in vases to drink for twenty-four hours before packing or travelling.

If you leave the foliage on the stem of a large exhibition flower, there is a great danger of damaging the lower florets when they rub on the top leaves during transit. Also, the flower tends to go limp because the foliage takes up most of the water. So the majority of large exhibition blooms seen on the show bench have two stems in the vase, one with leaves on and the other carrying the bloom. If the foliage stems are kept in water for a couple of days, they will travel on the car floor, without water.

Transporting methods are the same as previously described, but make absolutely sure that they are well fastened to the rods, or carried in the drums or vases in a perfectly upright position, for the very heavy heads soon lose their symmetry if held at an angle.

Medium exhibitions
These may be treated exactly as large exhibitions, but are usually shown with just a cane support fastened to the stem and with their own foliage, provided that it does not rub against the lower florets.

Singles
Because of the delicacy of their florets and the ease with which they get dislodged from the horizontal line, singles are transported with a circle of card (the same diameter as the flower), supporting the florets. It is held in position by a spring clothes-peg on the stem, just below the card.

The Schedule

By the time you reach the show, you should have studied your schedule and should know just which blooms you have for which classes. Check and check again that you are right; quite often I have seen experienced exhibitors put an incurve into an intermediate class, or a large into a medium class, or even put eight blooms in a class that only calls for seven.

Dressing

Unpack as soon as you can and get the blooms into water-filled vases. If you have brought spare blooms, select the most even fives or threes for your exhibits. Before vasing, tidy up the blooms with a petal roller, a couple of cotton-wool buds, a biro end, a small brush or finger and thumb. Be careful not to bruise, or you will be down-pointed. Tidy up the centres of the reflexes, leaving the contrasting circular button of undeveloped florets to stand out distinctively. Remove cleanly any florets which are spotted, damaged or way out of line (a good pair of tweezers is required for this job).

This dressing operation is necessary to show the flower off to its full potential, but do not go too far by combing out those reflexes that normally come with whorling florets. These may be just tidied up, for the judge has the power to down-point if the blooms are out of character.

Staging

Staging five blooms in a vase can be a very testing and trying experience. A piece of newspaper packed in the bottom of the vase provides a non-slip base for the stem ends. If the blooms are not perfectly matched, select the largest and deepest for the centre back and cut to about 700mm (27½in) in length. If you have to travel with shorter stems than this, a piece of thin galvanised wire pushed up the end of the stem will lengthen it quite easily. The two side back blooms go in next, 25mm (1in) shorter. The two front ones (the smallest) are 37 or 50mm (1½ or 2in) shorter again. Adjust the stems finally by packing with moss, or paper topped off with moss. The front two blooms and the top two-thirds of the back three blooms should be easily seen by judge and public. You should be able to put at least a finger between each bloom and its neighbour.

If you are showing in a multi-vase class, all the other vases must be at an identical height and staged in a similar manner. In these classes, put the smaller cultivars at the front and arrange the colours and types to make an exhibit that will attract the judge initially on presentation alone.

Large exhibitions
These are vased up after the foliage stems have been attached to the bloom stems. Use other exhibits as a guideline to staging heights; I like to stage about 510mm (20in) high. You should have a few good leaves below the bloom, spilling over on to the vase top. If you wish to broaden a flower, its ring can be pushed up, but this decreases the depth. The majority of large and medium exhibitions are staged one flower to a vase.

A major fault with a large exhibition bloom is lack of freshness on the lower florets, so if there is any sign of this when you are staging, remove the offending florets cleanly. Once the exhibit is staged, ease florets gently into place to present an even form or outline, and tidy up the reflexes around the top to give a clean and symmetrical shoulder.

Stage carefully and be meticulous in your presentation. Label your cultivars, make sure your exhibitor's card is in position, hope for the best, wish your fellow exhibitors all the best, and leave it to the judges. If you get a red ticket, be proud of your flowers and aim to do better next season; but if you do not win, take your defeat gracefully. Congratulate the winner, do not criticise the judge, and make a mental note to try even harder next year.

Final Advice

If you wish to become really interested in chrysanthemums, I recommend that you become a Fellow of the National Chrysanthemum Society. I can enrol you or let you have full details; just send a stamped addressed envelope to 'Saas-Fee', Crabtree Hill, Collingham, Wetherby, West Yorkshire. I will be only too pleased to help with any other problems. I can also send a copy of *Stopping Times* (price 80p inc postage), or write to W. B. Wade, 34 Gledhow Wood Grove, Leeds LS8 1NZ.

I sincerely hope that I have whetted your appetite or given you something to think about, for there is no secret in producing good exhibition blooms. It is just common sense, attention to detail and an unfading determination to win on the show bench. Happy growing and successful exhibiting.

8 The Chrysanthemum Grower's Calendar

Chrysanthemums provide interest and activity week by week throughout the year. The following suggestions will help to give you an orderly routine, prevent oversights, and keep your aims in mind. The calendar is compiled for growers in the centre of the British Isles; dates will be a little earlier in the North, and later in the South.

January

House further early stools, introduce to heat and moisture. Watch for aphids and slugs on cuttings. Insert large exhibition cuttings, and others which need early stops (in different sections). (Insert about 15–16 weeks ahead of stopping date.)
Prepare and mix John Innes No1 compost for first pottings or boxing of earlies.
Wash plant pots and boxes in a mild solution of Jeyes Fluid. Study the record books, think about the targets ahead and plan your methods.
Pot up the first of the rooted cuttings and stand them on the bench very close together.

February

Insert the main batch of late cuttings: incurved, reflexed, intermediate and singles. Shade from strong sunshine with butter muslin or newspaper.
Prepare more compost for first and second pottings. Wash intermediate plant pots. Continue to pot cuttings as they become rooted. Space out plants on the bench to give more light and air.
Prepare and clean outside frames for the earlies or lates. Check frame lights and clean the glass.
Check stocks of fertilisers, insecticides and canes, etc.
Mix John Innes No2 compost for earlies in base of the frame. If ash is to be used in early frames, make sure it has been weathered.
Don't water potted plants too soon; wait until they are showing a slight limpness in the morning.
Put late sprays to root to make stock plants.

March

Root early sprays. Check further rooting needs.
Double dig the early plot and incorporate well-rotted farmyard manure if

62

no winter digging was done. If winter dug, fork over as soon as the soil is workable.

Pot on the first large exhibition plants into intermediate pots and transfer into the frames.

Where earlies are bedded out in frames, plant at 150mm (6in) spacings in 75mm (3in) of compost. Only open frame lights in favourable conditions. Prepare to protect frames from frost with sacking, etc.

Water young plants only when the compost and plants are on the dry side. Give air to lates in frames whenever possible.

Box up late sprays.

April

Box up early sprays into John Innes No1 compost and take into frames. Keep a watch for aphids and commence spraying routines. Keep an eye on stopping dates. Pot up or pot on all cultivars when ready and transfer to frames. Mix final compost for lates. Respace pot plants in frames to avoid overcrowding. Provide a stick for all lates and fasten with rings. Don't expose plants to wind or rain, lift lights so that air can circulate. Apply base dressing to early plot and fork in – keep off if the soil is wet. If weather conditions are bad, consider covering the bed. Watch plant health. Pot-grown earlies may require planting out, so check the bed.

May

Most of the stopping will be done this month. Wash final pots and crocks. Check that the compost has correct moisture content. Pot on the first batch of large exhibitions and stand them outside, close together. Be prepared to protect from frost and heavy rain. Plant out earlies and early sprays, making sure they are watered previously. Secure to canes. Prepare the standing ground and straining wires for the lates. Continue final potting of lates when they have filled the second pot with roots. Only water when the plants reach the point of obvious need. Stop early sprays towards the end of the month.

June

Keep the early plot weed free and hoe between plants. Thin out breaks as soon as the required number can be secured to supporting canes. Keep a watchful eye for codling-moth larvae. Position lates on the standing ground, insert canes and fasten to straining wires.

Commence overhead spraying to earlies and lates when the sun is hot.
Make a thorough weekly inspection of every plant.
Commence feeds to lates five weeks after final potting.
Watch for aphids and keep up spraying routines.
Give supplementary dressing of fertiliser to earlies if the bed is fairly new.
Hoe and water in.
Cut off sucker growth on earlies or lates. Put to root if small stock plants are required.
Thin down early sprays to four even breaks.
Carry out second-crown stops.

July

Put late sprays to root in closed pit (consider Jiffy 7s).
Observe watering routines.
Space laterals evenly on lates; reduce to desired crop plus one spare.
Keep secured to canes as growth develops.
As the buds of earlies appear, begin to remove growths and buds surrounding them.
Check that covers and bloom-bags are ready for use.
Commence gradual reduction of spare large-exhibition laterals.
Watch for earwig damage and use thick wire to destroy them in the cane tops.
Place double bud-bags on earlies (at calyx split) before covers go on.
Watch for mildew and spray with Benlate or Nimrod T.
Continue feeding lates.
When rooted, pot late sprays into 127mm (5in) pots using John Innes No2 compost.
Remove the centre bud on early-spray laterals, when large enough, and restrict other buds to five, six, seven or eight.

August

Put late sprays into finals using John Innes No2 compost.
Secure buds of large exhibitions during the next two or three weeks.
Cover and bag earlies; protect sides of the bed from wind and rain.
Change over to bud feed on lates, after securing.
Secure buds of other types of lates within the next few weeks.
Check show dates and transporting equipment.
Keep a watch for earwigs and aphids in early blooms.
Black out late sprays for a three-week period, seventy days before the show date.

September

Cut off spare laterals before housing (all except large exhibitions).
Cease feeding lates before colour shows.
Prepare the greenhouse for lates as they are ready for housing. Shade on

the sun side to keep temperatures down.

Double bud-bag lates (on calyx split), but house them and remove bags before the florets get too long.

Keep the greenhouse fully ventilated.

Secure buds of late singles.

After early exhibiting, mark selected plants for next year's stock.

Continue housing lates after calyx split.

Remove central buds on late sprays; feed and water. Watch for mildew on them, especially after blackout treatment.

October

Take late sprays into the greenhouse and give a little warmth.

Prepare John Innes No1 compost for early stools.

Inspect lates and remove any marked florets.

Keep air moving and put heat on when nights are damp and still.

Try to keep the temperature in the greenhouse at night a few degrees above outside temperature. Keep bottom vents open, but close top vents if overhead heating is used.

Trim basal growth on lates to provide cutting material eight weeks later.

Cut down footstalks on earlies; keep the covers on; dig up and destroy any poor plants.

Prepare frame for early stools and check supply of boxes.

Check show dates and transporting equipment.

November

Lift early stools and box into John Innes No1 compost, transfer to cold frames.

Order farmyard manure if not already done.

Carry out stock selection of lates.

Cut down lates and leave in pots, or trim roots into squares and box.

Keep early stools cool and airy, but protect from frost and soaking with rain.

After the last show, reduce the minimum greenhouse temperature to just over freezing point.

Dig and manure early bed if soil is heavy and on the clay side.

December

Clean greenhouse glass and remove all shading.

Erect propagating pit and check soil-warming cables.

Take early stools from the frames and put on to warming cables. Water them when they have warmed up.

Around Christmas, increase the minimum temperature to 5°C (40°F).

Put to root some large exhibition cultivars.

Order next season's new cultivars.

Indulge in thoughtful revision of the year and plan for better results.

Glossary

Break (or lateral) Side growth. To break is to branch or to send out side growth. Natural breaks are side growths appearing on the main stem after the break bud has formed.

Break bud Flower bud which, if the plant is left to grow naturally, appears at the end of the solitary main stem, before it branches or breaks. In normal circumstances this bud shrivels and does not develop a flower.

Bud-bag Greaseproof-paper bag used to protect buds after calyx split, until replaced by a larger bag or the plants go into the greenhouse. Double bud-bags are used (one inside the other) when there is no overhead protection.

Bud initiation When the plant starts to produce a bud.

Calyx Outer covering of a flower bud, which splits to reveal the florets.

Compost For potting, this is a mixture of loam, peat, and grit or perlite, to which certain plant foods have been added in order to produce a suitable medium for growing plants in pots.

Counting down The process of cutting out all breaks in excess of those required for the crop.

Covers Polythene sheets, or polythene-covered or glazed frames, erected over an early bed for bloom protection.

Crocks Broken pieces of clay plant pot, which are placed concave side downwards over drainage holes in plant pots.

Cultivar An internationally agreed term for a plant variant raised in a garden as a seedling or sport.

Cutting Unrooted leafy growth, taken from the old root or stem.

Damping Decay and rotting of the flower before maturity, caused by close humid conditions, still air and lack of ventilation.

First-crown bud The first bud which appears at the end of a lateral growth from the main stem of the plant. It is a natural first crown when the plant has made a natural break; as distinct from one which appears on a plant that has been stopped, ie had the tip of the main stem removed before the break bud has formed.

Florets Ray florets are the outer florets of the flower, usually large with colourful petals, fused to form a broad, strap-like structure. Disc florets are the central florets of the flower, usually small with yellow petals, fused into a short tube, as in the centre of singles.

No-soil compost Mixture of peat with grit or perlite, and plant foods.

pH Acidity scale: pH 7.0 is the neutral point, pH values below 7.0 denote increasing acidity and values above 7.0 denote increasing alkalinity.

Perlite Expanded particles of volcanic rock, used in modern potting composts.

Pedicel Small stalk joining a flower or flower cluster to the main stem.

Propagation Plant multiplication by asexual means, eg cuttings.

Running on The process of rubbing out the first- or second-crown bud and allowing the next shoot down the stem to grow on and develop a flower.

Seagold Calcified seaweed possessing natural trace elements.

Second-crown bud If the tips of the lateral growths from the main stem are removed (ie if the first breaks are stopped), further side growths develop in the leaf axils of these laterals. These further side growths (second breaks) then grow on (perhaps for 600mm/2ft) until a bud is produced at the end of each of them. That bud is the second-crown bud.

Securing a bud Removing all side shoots and unwanted buds and leaving only the bud which is to develop into a flower.

Side shoots Small growths emerging from the leaf joints.

Spit A spade depth.

Sport A change which sometimes occurs in an established cultivar. The change may be in the colour, form or shape of the flower, the vigour or habit of the plant, or the normal flowering date.

Spray Last flowering growth consisting of one stem (not a branch), with or without a central flower or bud.

Stool The root of an old plant, with a portion of the old stem and its surrounding young shoots.

Stopping (or pinching) Removing the tip of the main stem or a side growth.

Top dressing Layer of potting compost spread on the surface of the soil.

Turgid State of leaves and flowers when fully inflated with water.

Vegetative Stage of plant growth without buds or flowers.

Vernalisation Subjecting the stools to cool temperatures.

Index

Figures in italic indicate illustrations